AN ILLUSTRATED GUIDE TO SELF-DISCIPLINE

50 Habits to More Self-Control, Success, and Satisfaction in Life

By Martin Meadows

TABLE OF CONTENTS

PROLOGUE

This isn't your typical self-help book.

It isn't meant to be read once and then thrown into a dark corner. Instead, it's designed to inspire you daily—to show you in an entertaining, vivid way how to cultivate self-discipline through powerful habits you can introduce in your life today.

You'll notice there's a cat or a dog in each illustration. Pets are cool, but it's not the reason why you'll see them on every page. They're there to symbolize everyday life.

The cat symbolizes the mundane or difficult. It symbolizes obstacles; people who laugh at your efforts, don't believe in you, or project their limiting beliefs on you. It also symbolizes prosaic day-to-day concerns. (Sorry cat lovers, a dog wouldn't fit this role.)

The dog symbolizes excitement, inspiration, and energy. It symbolizes when everything goes right, when you're in the flow, when you're motivated, when people share your vision and support you.

Our imperfect lives consist of interweaving cat and dog moments. Ups and downs. Triumphs and failures. Memorable moments and humdrum hustle. Amid it all, you need to demonstrate your commitment to self-discipline every day, as that's how you can change your life to attract more success and fulfillment.

Before you turn the page, one last thing...Promise yourself that you'll try at the very least 10 habits from this book.

If you work with a fitness coach, you don't just chat with them. You do the exercises and follow their dietary recommendations.

Treat this book the same way. Pick one habit and follow it for a few weeks. If you're happy with the benefits it gives you, keep it in your life and choose another to work on.

Please talk with your physician before you try some of the habits from this book. Safety should always be your first concern. I'm NOT a qualified physician, psychotherapist, or any other accredited expert. All the habits are presented for informational and motivational purposes only.

HABIT #1: A HABIT TO RULE THEM ALL. TRACK HABITS.

The other habits I'll present in this book are like a buffet menu—pick whatever you like in no particular order. This habit is the price of admission: you must pay if you want to enjoy the other selections.

Create a habit tracking system that spells out what you're going to do and how often. Don't merely keep track in your head. When your habits aren't written down, they don't feel real. I can't emphasize this enough: you absolutely need a tracking system to help you implement new habits.

Your system doesn't have to be complex. I use a simple spreadsheet and put "x" on each day I engage in a daily habit and each week I engage in a weekly habit. You can use an app on your phone or a good old-fashioned journal. Whatever you choose, use it every day.

Define your habit in specific, measurable terms, for example: "I jog for 30 minutes, three times a week" or "I save $50 every week."

HABIT TRACKING

MONDAY	TUESDAY	WEDNESDAY
PROTEIN DAY		RUNNING 40 MIN
COLD SHO'ER	RUNNING 30 MIN	

FRIDAY	RDAY	SUNDAY
		PROTEIN DAY
PROTEIN DAY		RUNNING 40 MIN
		COLD SHOWER

7

HABIT #2: PREPARE YOURSELF. FOLLOW A MORNING RITUAL.

A morning ritual is a routine you engage in every morning that helps you start the day off on the right note. *The goal is to boost your energy, get inspired, and prepare yourself for the tasks ahead.*

It can involve: a brief workout (pushups, jumping jacks, squats, burpees—anything that improves your blood circulation), breathing exercises, planning your main tasks, visualizing a favorable outcome of today's activities, expressing gratitude, and revising your long-term plans.

Create it any way you want, but make sure that it conditions your mind to be positive, disciplined, and outcome-oriented.

HABIT #3: MODERATION VS ABSTINENCE. IDENTIFY YOUR STYLE OF SELF-DISCIPLINE.

Bestselling author Gretchen Rubin proposes that there are two types of people: moderators and abstainers. Moderators are more successful with their resolutions when they allow themselves an occasional treat. Meanwhile, abstainers prefer to commit themselves 100%, with no exceptions, as they're unable to use moderation.

For example, if you want to lose weight and you know that even a single scoop of ice cream makes you devour the contents of every container in sight, you should follow the strategy of an abstainer. Ice cream has to disappear from your diet with no exceptions.

If, however, you go crazy without an occasional ice cream treat—and it really is just a scoop every other week—then you're a moderator. In this case, you need some treats to achieve success.

When forming new habits, always identify which approach you should take and set rules that will help you stick to them. Like tracking habits, this is another meta-habit that will help you become more successful in establishing new routines.

HABIT #4: STAY CALM, COOL, AND COLLECTED. EMBRACE INCONVENIENCES.

When you find yourself in an inconvenient situation, instead of getting frustrated, say "Great! Now I can…" and look on the bright side. *By staying calm, cool, and collected in an inconvenient situation, you build the ability to stay disciplined under pressure.*

For example, if you're waiting in a long line, you can say "Great! Now I can practice my patience." If it's raining and you wanted to head out for a run, you can say: "Great! Now I can practice my physical skills and my mental fortitude."

For additional practice, expose yourself to minor inconveniences on purpose. This way, you'll train yourself to better handle similar non-voluntary situations in the future. For example, be 15 minutes early to a meeting and pretend that the other person is late. *How can you control your growing impatience? What's the bright side?*

HABIT #5: NURTURE YOUR BODY. EAT A BIG PORTION OF VEGETABLES.

Health is one of the most important things in life. Yet, few people follow the most fundamental nutritional principle that could dramatically improve their well-being and by extension, their performance in all aspects of life.

This piece of advice is to eat vegetables every day. Veggies are full of nutrients, have few calories compared to processed foods, and are more filling. They energize your body, help you maintain healthy weight, and reduce the risk of health disorders.

Eating a half to a full pound of vegetables a day is a powerful far-reaching habit that will improve your health and positively impact other aspects of your life.

HABIT #6: BOOST YOUR MIND. EXPRESS GRATITUDE.

You can be worth billions, yet still be miserable if you miss one crucial element: gratitude. People who appreciate what they have, no matter how little it is, are happier and live more fulfilling lives.

Maintaining a positive attitude trains your willpower because optimism comes down to conditioning your mind. *It's you who chooses to indulge in negative thoughts or feel grateful even if things aren't going well.*

Each day, take a minute or two to express appreciation. Consistent practice will retrain your brain to focus on what's right instead of what's wrong. This will help you pursue your goals and persist despite obstacles you'll encounter along the way.

HABIT #7: BUILD CONFIDENCE. TRY PUBLIC SPEAKING.

Getting in front of a group of people and giving a talk is uncomfortable, to say the least. Which is why public speaking is such a good exercise for self-discipline.

It teaches you how to maintain composure in a stressful situation. This boosts your emotional control and helps you better deal with temptations and impulses. *Public speaking also builds your confidence and leadership skills.*

This has a big impact on your self-discipline, showing you that embracing some discomfort in life pays big dividends. Consider joining a Toastmasters group or volunteer for public speaking at work. *Don't avoid opportunities to speak in front of people in your personal life, too.*

HABIT #8: BECOME A PRODUCER. CREATE MORE THAN YOU CONSUME.

Work takes self-discipline, while consumption is indulgence. Both are important in life, but for the purpose of growth and happiness, strive to produce far more than you consume. This has an effect not only on your financial life, but also overall personal fulfillment.

Do your best instead of cutting corners. Share your work with the world. Volunteer to be a leader. Organize events and parties. Introduce people to each other. Give thoughtful advice. *Offer support.*

When you focus on creating value, you become a professional value adder and problem solver. This gives you the opportunity to become more resourceful, a trait that will help you accomplish your own goals, too.

HABIT #9: OVERCOME PROCRASTINATION. DO IT NOW.

If you always postpone uncomfortable activities, you train yourself to prioritize instant, insignificant rewards. This is the opposite of what you need if you want to become more disciplined.

Procrastination gives you some enjoyment today at the expense of more substantial benefits tomorrow. For example, you watch your favorite TV show today at the expense of high stress tomorrow, trying to finish an important presentation last minute.

Whenever you catch yourself saying "I'll do it later," stop whatever you're doing and get to work. No matter how tempting it feels today, putting things off guarantees a less pleasant future. Consistent training this way will help you establish a habit of engaging in the unpleasant and uncomfortable today, so you can enjoy a more pleasant, positive, and promising tomorrow.

23

HABIT #10: KEEP THINGS IN ORDER. MAKE YOUR BED.

In his University of Texas at Austin 2014 Commencement Address, Admiral William H. McRaven said:

"If you make your bed every morning, you will have accomplished the first task of the day. It will give you a small sense of pride, and it will encourage you to do another task, and another, and another. And by the end of the day that one task completed will have turned into many tasks completed."

Making your bed in the morning helps you become more conscientious. You program yourself to refuse sloppiness and embrace high standards. This carries over to how you conduct yourself throughout the rest of the day.

HABIT #11: ERADICATE NEGATIVITY. QUIT COMPLAINING.

Complaining is nothing but mental laziness: instead of cutting out unproductive negative thoughts, you choose to indulge in them. This changes nothing except for ruining your mood.

Each time you begin to complain, consider it an exercise in willpower. *Change your focus to something positive.* If the weather is bad, at least you have a roof over your head. If you're still waiting for your meal after ordering it thirty minutes ago, at least you can afford to eat out.

Additionally, instead of wasting your time complaining about a recurrent annoying situation, think of potential solutions. For example, if you abhor your commute, perhaps it's time to move closer to your workplace, negotiate working from home, or find a new job.

Switching complaints to productive thoughts will help you improve your mental discipline and teach you to look for solutions instead of exhibiting negativity.

HABIT #12: LEARN THROUGH PRACTICE. SET A BIG CHALLENGE.

Challenges are like sculpting tools for self-discipline. While working on a big goal that tests your resolve in a specific area, you improve your discipline in this particular thing, as well as in other aspects of your life.

Success breeds success. Each challenge you undertake offers lessons that will help in your future endeavors. Pursue a big challenge regularly. Some examples include:

- running/biking/swimming/walking, etc. for a long distance during a specific time period, e.g. running 1000 miles over three months.

- performing x total number of reps this month, e.g. 1000 pushups.

- fundraising $50,000 this year for your favorite charity.

- becoming a fluent speaker in a foreign language in two years.

- acquiring any difficult skill as a long-term project.

HABIT #13: LIVE BY YOUR RULES. IDENTIFY NON-NEGOTIABLES.

Get disciplined by establishing rules that can't be broken under any circumstances. A clear set of principles will serve as a roadblock against impulse decisions that jeopardize your future.

For example, one of your non-negotiables could be that you can't get too comfortable. Each week, you need to engage in something that scares, challenges, or otherwise helps you grow. This rule will protect you from resting on your laurels, and consequently, losing self-discipline.

When establishing your unbreakable rules, evaluate whether you live your life according to them. If there's incongruity, use it as a source of motivation so that your life reflects your most important principles.

If one of your non-negotiables is that you absolutely need to do whatever is in your power to take care of your family, wouldn't finally losing the excess pounds help you fulfill this role?

If one of your rules is to prioritize free time over material goods, wouldn't it make sense to improve your productivity, so you can spend more time with your loved ones?

HABIT #14: INSPIRE YOURSELF DAILY. CREATE EVERYDAY VISUAL REMINDERS.

Recommitting to your goals every day is key to consistent motivation. One of the best ways to do so is through everyday visual reminders: images, videos, quotes, items or music that reminds you why you're pursuing your goal.

Here are some ideas:
1. Use an image that represents your dream future as a wallpaper on your device.

2. Put a picture of your desired outcome somewhere where you will see it multiple times a day (for example on the fridge).

3. Print inspiring pictures and quotes and pin them to a corkboard by your desk.

4. Set a daily reminder on your phone with a quick message such as: "I eat healthily," "I'm joyful all the time," "I make decisions that favor my future."

5. Put a small item on your nightstand that reminds you of what your goal will help you escape from. For example, a small clock will inspire you to work on your business by reminding you that you no longer want to wake up with an alarm.

HABIT #15: BROADEN YOUR HORIZONS. READ BOOKS.

If you browse through interviews with some of the most successful people, they all seem to share the same habit: *they're avid readers.*

Reading books—whether it's a novel, an autobiography, or a how-to guide—broadens your horizons. **When you gain new perspectives, you challenge your existing beliefs and embrace a new outlook on life.**

In addition to that, reading regularly manifests your devotion to continuous education, a value that every successful person espouses in everyday life.

I strongly suggest reading autobiographies of people you admire. It's the easiest way to get inside the mind of a person you'd like to emulate and apply their ideas in your own life.

HABIT #16: BE BRAVE. FACE YOUR FEARS.

When you willingly subject yourself to something you fear, your willpower muscle is stretched in the same way as when you seek little inconveniences and decide to stay calm amid frustration. *It comes down to acclimatizing yourself to discomfort—in this case fear—which makes you more resilient when facing hardships.*

Identify your fears and periodically face them to grow your willpower muscle and courage. Do it safely, though. This isn't about heading out to the Amazon rainforest by yourself to overcome your fear of snakes. *Think how you can gradually lessen your fear in a safe and controlled environment.*

HABIT #17: BEFRIEND HUNGER. PRACTICE INTERMITTENT FASTING.

Intermittent fasting is a pattern of eating in which you abstain from food for at least 14-16 hours. It's yet another exercise that will test your resolve by putting yourself in a self-inflicted uncomfortable situation. *This time, you're testing your willpower by exposing yourself to hunger.*

In addition to being a great exercise to toughen up, fasting is healthy, with many benefits documented by scientific research. *Fasting also makes you more flexible in life.* If you can go without eating for a prolonged period of time, you don't have to schedule your life around meals.

The easiest way to practice intermittent fasting is by skipping breakfast. You can also stop eating a few hours before going to sleep or set an eating window, for example you only eat between 11 am and 7 pm. If you're up for a bigger challenge, fast for 24 hours or more.

HABIT #18: DEFEAT DISTRACTIONS. MEDITATE.

Distractions abound in today's fast-paced world. It's a constant struggle to maintain focus. To make matters worse, getting away from it all isn't easy as you're always a finger tap away from your smartphone.

That's where meditation can help. *Meditation is about reducing your focus to a single thing.* There's no need to sit cross-legged, though. You can focus on your breath, a candle flame, an incantation, hitting the tennis ball, putting one foot in front of another, sparring in a boxing gym, climbing, surfing, dancing tango, writing, painting, and any other activity that requires your full focus to perform well.

Regularly spending time in a meditative state will improve your ability to concentrate. With increased control over your mind, you'll become more disciplined in all areas of your life.

HABIT #19: BE HONEST.
TELL THE TRUTH.

Defaulting to comfortable choices often brings more problems than benefits. Lying is an example of such a choice, which, at first, is a more comfortable choice than being honest, but ultimately comes at a steep price. *When discovered, a lie breaks trust, and sometimes even relationships—all for an impulsive decision to save yourself some discomfort.*

Telling the truth can be distressing, but as long as you're civilized about it, most people will appreciate and admire your frankness. *Mastering honesty will improve your relationships and make you more in control when it comes to using self-discipline in a social setting.*

43

HABIT #20: STRAIGHTEN UP. KEEP A GOOD POSTURE.

Eliminating little bad habits from your everyday life is an easy way to improve willpower. One of these habits is keeping a poor posture: slouching in a chair, leaning on one leg, hunching over a computer, rounding your shoulders or cradling a phone to your ear.

Develop awareness of your posture and correct it throughout the day. *In addition to improving your willpower, your back will thank you.*

As a reminder to keep a good posture, put a sticky note at eye-level on the door frame of your kitchen, bedroom, or any other room you pass through regularly.

HABIT #21: MOOD IS A CHOICE. CONTROL YOUR MENTAL STATE.

Your physiology affects your mental state on a deep level.

Try it now: stand up, put a bright smile on your face, and start jumping up and down. You'll feel energized and happier. Now round your shoulders, frown, and stare at your feet while tensing your back. Not an easy position to be happy in, right?

While you can't eliminate negative events from your life, you can control your response to them. Nobody is forcing you to feel bad. Bad emotions are sometimes useful, but they shouldn't be the norm.

Use negative states as a trigger to work on your emotional control. **Smile. Think grateful thoughts.** Change your body language to feel more positive. Strive to be a cheerful, supportive person. Focus on helping others feel good, and you'll feel good, too.

Create a list of things you can do to make yourself feel better. Whenever you feel negative, pick one thing to lift your spirits.

A side note: if you think you're depressed, please, please talk with a qualified therapist. Don't put it off. Go and schedule a consultation now. ***You don't have to go it alone.***

47

HABIT #22: GET MORE ENERGY. WAKE UP EARLY.

Waking up early will improve your life in two ways. *First, you'll practice your willpower.* It's not an easy feat to demonstrate self-discipline when you're still half-asleep. *Second, waking up early gives you a head start and helps you be more productive.*

The evening before, plan something exciting or pleasant to do in the morning. If you don't have anything to look forward to in the morning, getting up will be difficult.

Plan to slowly enjoy a cup of coffee or tea, jog while listening to your favorite music, learn something interesting, read a book by your favorite author, or work on an exciting project.

If you aren't an early riser, follow a routine that works for you. *Waking up early doesn't work for everybody, but everybody can benefit from a regular, predictable schedule.*

49

HABIT #23: FEEL GOOD FEELING BAD. TAKE COLD SHOWERS.

If you're looking for a simple way to test and grow your willpower, look no further than your bathroom. *Turn the cold water on and enjoy the pleasures of frigid water hitting your body.*

By taking a cold shower when the hot water is available, you put yourself in a self-imposed inconvenient situation. You learn how to tolerate unpleasant circumstances in a safe environment from which you can escape whenever it gets too difficult to handle.

This habit will help you toughen up and improve your ability to grin and bear short-term intense discomfort.

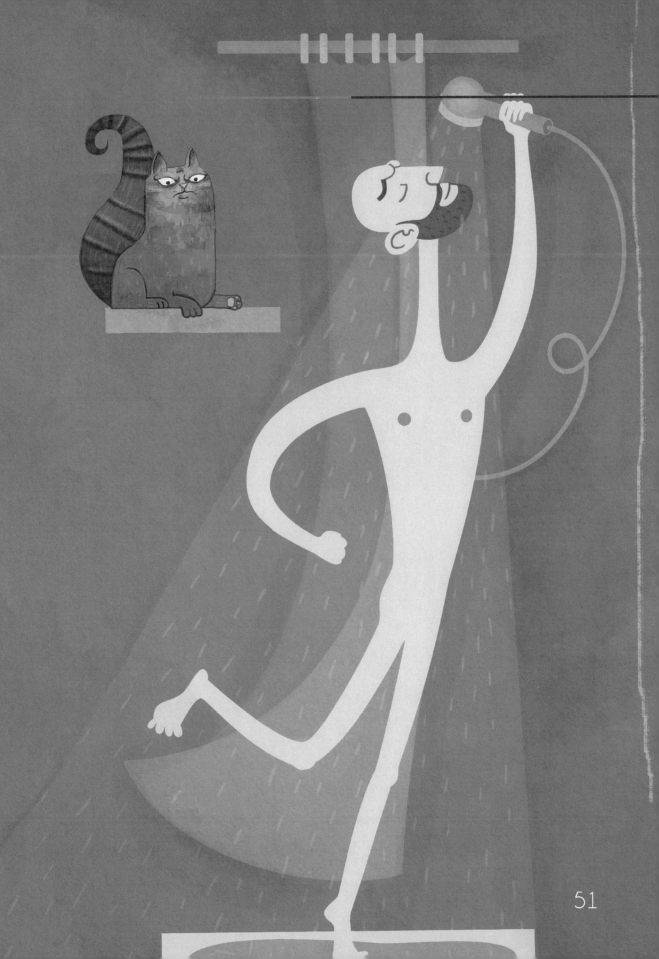

HABIT #24: DO IT ANYWAY.
EMBRACE THE SUCK.

In his book *Living with a Seal*, author Jesse Itzler quotes the following words of his coach, Navy SEAL David Goggins: *"if it doesn't suck, we don't do it."*

Doing things that suck is the opposite of what a sane person would prefer to do, yet it's the key differentiator between a disciplined and weak-willed person.

The natural reaction to difficulties and obstacles is to make excuses and evade them. *If you run away from things that suck, however, you lose the opportunity to train yourself to handle hardships.*

It's more pleasant and comfortable to seek easy things, but doing what's difficult helps you grow the most. For example, running in ideal conditions is fun. *Running when it's cold, rainy, humid, or otherwise difficult, is what builds your character the most, though.*

When working on your objectives, don't be afraid to seek what's difficult. That's where you can learn the most. Often, a single highly challenging experience can teach you more than weeks of engaging in what's easy.

HABIT #25: BOOST YOUR RESOLVE. ACKNOWLEDGE YOUR LITTLE WINS.

If determination enables you to travel toward your goals, then acknowledging your wins is like refueling this vehicle along the way. *People who don't acknowledge their little wins may fail to notice progress and subsequently, lose motivation to keep going.*

You don't have to score huge wins to congratulate yourself for a job well done. In fact, most of the time it's consistent little achievements that produce big successes.

If you're on a diet, congratulate yourself for eating vegetables, drinking a smoothie, or refusing an unhealthy meal. If you want to improve your financial situation, feel good that you saved $10 today or that your side gig helps you make an additional $100 a month.

Acknowledge your little wins every day. When reviewing each week, don't forget to congratulate yourself for continuous dedication to your goals.

HABIT #26: OPEN YOUR MIND. BRAINSTORM.

A habit of black-and-white thinking impairs your ability to make changes. If you believe you have only two options, you'll most likely choose to keep things the same. As they say, the devil you know is better than an unknown angel. Challenging your beliefs by refusing to see only two options and always brainstorming alternatives will help you escape this dangerous type of thinking.

For example, most people assume that there are only two choices when it comes to pursuing their entrepreneurial dreams: you either start a business and risk losing it all or keep the job you hate and shelve your entrepreneurial plans.

Now take a person who refuses to think in black and white. It turns out that there are more than two options: they can keep their job and work on their business in the mornings, partner up with somebody to share responsibilities, ask their boss to work part-time, switch to a contract, pursue venture capital so they can start with adequate resources, and so on.

Resist lazy thinking. There's always a third option, and often a fourth, fifth or sixth one.

HABIT #27: MAKE SPACE FOR WHAT MATTERS. DECLUTTER.

Physical clutter is not only unpleasant to look at, but also affects your ability to concentrate. Keeping things neat and tidy requires self-discipline, which provides an opportunity to exercise your willpower muscle. *Decluttering is also a fantastic way to clear your mind of distractions and regain focus.*

Discard things like worn out clothes, gadgets you don't use, and items that you should have thrown out a long time ago like old cardboard boxes and expired products. *Apply decluttering to your electronic life, too.* Don't keep dozens of tabs open in your browser. Don't put a seventieth icon on your desktop. Don't install another trendy app on your phone.

Identify what items contribute little to your life and reduce them to the bare minimum. For example, if you don't particularly care about clothes, simplify your wardrobe and donate clothes you rarely wear.

Keep clutter at bay by taking a quick assessment each week and regularly discarding things you no longer need.

HABIT #28: MAINTAIN MOMENTUM. ALWAYS TAKE A STEP FORWARD.

Getting started is often the hardest part. Once you put the machine in motion, keep it running. Form a habit that, no matter what, you'll always take at least a tiny action related to your goals. It's unrealistic to expect that you'll always be on top of your game, but you can always do something to manifest your commitment.

For example, if you don't feel like exercising, tell yourself that you'll exercise for only one minute and then you'll be done. Even if that's all you'll do today, you'll still take a little step forward and maintain some momentum. *Thanks to this, tomorrow you won't wake up thinking that since you already skipped your routine yesterday, you can skip it today, too.*

HABIT #29: OPTIMIZE ENERGY LEVELS. CONTROL CAFFEINE.

Caffeine is a godsend for go-getters. Unfortunately, there's no free lunch. You can't artificially maintain high energy all the time. *Caffeine can be helpful if you need a jolt of energy, but if you consume it daily just to get through the day, it leads to an addiction.* Instead of giving you a burst of energy, caffeine becomes something that you must consume to keep yourself from falling over.

Too much caffeine leads to headaches, irritability, restlessness, and nervousness, none of which are conducive to self-discipline. To make matters worse, consuming caffeine six hours before bed reduces sleep quality, making you even more tired the next day.

Is caffeine the devil that has absolutely no place in your life? Obviously not. Could you benefit by controlling your caffeine intake? Absolutely.

Consider switching coffee with herbal tea and trying caffeine-free coffee alternatives like chicory coffee. *Stop drinking energy drinks altogether, that, unlike coffee, provide no health benefits and pose a big risk to your health.*

tea °o

COFFEE

63

HABIT #30: GAIN STRENGTH. PUSH YOUR PHYSICAL LIMITS.

Regular physical activity is one of the most powerful habits—not only because it's vital to health, but also because it's an excellent opportunity to practice your willpower.

Each time you perform a difficult exercise despite discomfort, you stretch your limits. Repeatedly pushing your physical limits builds your physical strength and mental fortitude at the same time.

Gently push your limits during most workouts. From time to time, push your limits—safely and mindfully—to a more extreme level. The keyword here is "your limits." **Don't compare yourself to others.** It doesn't matter if you can't run for more than two minutes while others run for hours. **Compete with yourself.**

HABIT #31: EFFORT BRINGS RESULTS. DRESS WELL.

Dressing well seems like a relic of the past. In today's egalitarian world, we should judge people based on their behavior, not how they dress. This statement makes sense, but it doesn't change the fact that we still react more positively to a well-dressed person than a sloppy dresser.

Dressing up is less comfortable than wearing your favorite casual clothes. However, as we've already established it, a little discomfort is often worth it. People who are well-dressed make a better first impression, look more professional, attractive, and confident. Your external appearance can have a big impact on how powerful you feel inside.

Should you wear a suit or a formal dress every day? Let's be realistic—you won't do it, and it isn't necessary. Should you make an effort to look your best—and feel okay with little discomfort—when pursuing an important person, attending an important meeting, or whenever you need a little boost of confidence? If you want it badly enough, the answer is clear.

HABIT #32: BE WELL-ROUNDED. WORK ON A WEAKNESS.

When you employ your strengths, you feel in control. You're doing what you're good at, and it always feels good when things go well. Conversely, if you work on your weaknesses, you don't feel comfortable. Frustrations abound. Challenges seem insurmountable.

There's a lot you can learn by periodically doing things you aren't good at. You train yourself to keep going despite virtually insurmountable obstacles. *You improve your patience when all you want to do is yell with frustration.* You become a well-rounded person.

Make a list of your weaknesses. Ask yourself which ones would benefit your life the most if you became better at them. Each month or quarter pick one to work on.

HABIT #33: RESTORE BALANCE.
CONNECT WITH NATURE.

We seek ways to become more disciplined, energized, efficient. Yet, sometimes what we need is the opposite. We need to restore balance by doing less and returning to our primal place in the world: nature.

Regularly spending time in a natural setting, whether it's a local park, beach, mountains, desert, forest, jungle, sea, lake, or ocean, is one of the best ways to recharge. *It will help you take care of your mental health and maintain maximum performance in the long run.*

Failing to turn down the dial and losing oneself in a noisy and distracting urban living is a sure-fire recipe for burnout. Ensure that you regularly recharge your batteries by spending a quiet hour or two in a natural, restorative setting.

HABIT #34: ENSURE YOU'RE ON THE RIGHT PATH. REVISE YOUR DIRECTION.

Self-discipline is a tool that can help you accomplish your goals. This tool is only useful, however, if you apply it to the right objectives.

Blind stubbornness while pursuing objectives you don't particularly care about anymore is wasteful. To make matters worse, if you don't regularly reflect on your life direction, the less important goals may rob you of the resources you should spend on other, more fundamental aspects of your life.

For example, in the blind pursuit of making more money you may sacrifice your relationships, a much more important value in your life.

Periodically revising your direction is a key preventative measure to check for any discrepancies between your lifestyle and your values. Ask yourself whether you still care about your goals. *Find out if your everyday habits are congruent with the direction you want to take.*

HABIT #35: KEEP IT SIMPLE. IDENTIFY YOUR ONE THING.

Described in detail in Gary Keller's and Jay Papasan's book *The One Thing*, the habit of identifying and focusing your resources on your *"one thing"* comes down to answering the following question:

"What's the one thing you can do such that by doing it everything else will be easier or unnecessary?"

Powerful self-discipline habits aren't merely about improving self-discipline: they're also about optimizing its use. Focusing on the most transformational activity will require less self-discipline. When setting a new goal, identify your one thing and double down on it to become more effective and successful while doing less.

HABIT #36: CREATE A NETWORK OF HABITS. DEVELOP MOTIVATIONAL LINKS.

A motivational link is a bridge between a new habit and your lifestyle: values, activities, people, existing habits, etc. *Developing motivational links for each new habit creates a strong, self-reinforcing network of habits.*

For example, you can engage in a new habit like stretching after brushing your teeth in the morning. *This way, each time you brush teeth, you remember about stretching.*

Another example of a motivational link is linking a new habit with your passion. Identify specific benefits of a new habit on your passion, like a healthy diet improving your performance in tennis. You can also combine your passion with a new habit, for example, by listening to educational podcasts while you run.

Lastly, you can develop a motivational link by linking a new habit with another person. You can implement a new habit with your spouse, friend, or a loved one, or link your new habit with the positive impact it will have on them. For example, a habit of saving 10% of your salary a month will greatly benefit your entire family. Making a clear connection between saving and caring for your family can give you a motivational boost to sustain this new habit.

HABIT #37: EMBRACE SOCIAL PRESSURE. MAKE NEW FRIENDS.

Research on social learning theory by Albert Bandura has shown that you can acquire new behaviors by observing and imitating others.

Surrounding yourself with people who exhibit traits you'd like to develop yourself is a shortcut you can use to your advantage to achieve goals more quickly. When you make friends with people relevant to your pursuits, you'll need less self-discipline to change because you'll adopt the right behaviors through mere social exposure.

For example, if you start going to the gym and make friends with frequent gymgoers, you'll find it easier to stick to your habit and exhibit values that will improve your fitness and health.

Since we copy behaviors, beliefs, and habits of people closest to us, we need to consciously choose our immediate environment. *Make sure it's working to your advantage.*

HABIT #38: FEEL BETTER. GET SOME SUNSHINE.

Vitamin D, a hormone the body produces when exposed to sun, improves bone health, protects from certain cancers, and has a positive impact on organs, muscles, autoimmune health, and the brain. It also elevates your sense of well-being, helps those suffering from seasonal affective disorder, and reduces premenstrual syndrome.

According to common knowledge, spending any amount of unprotected time in the sun is dangerous. The experts say that you should avoid going outside between 11 am and 3 pm and always wear sunscreen.

Unfortunately, the sun's angle before 11 am and after 3 pm is too low to make your body synthetize vitamin D. Wearing sunscreen all the time decreases your body's ability to synthetize vitamin D by over 90%. This leads to a large percentage of people being deficient in this important vitamin.

Supplementation can help, but it doesn't have the same effects as the sun. *The best way to produce sufficient vitamin D is to get at least one hour a week of unprotected sun exposure between 11 am and 3 pm.*

Regularly exposing yourself to sun for optimal levels of the all-important vitamin D will boost your mood, ensure that you're healthy, and by extension, help you become more successful.

81

HABIT #39: SLOW DOWN. TAKE A FEW DAYS OFF.

Rest is just as important as work. If you're exhausted, you're unlikely to get anything done. Making sure that your body and mind have a chance to recover is vital to your goals.

Designate regular rest periods: a scheduled block of time reserved for you and you alone. Spend it meditating, having a nap, listening to your favorite music, taking a walk, reading, or anything else that relaxes you.

If you've been working with more intensity than usual, you should spend more time in recovery, too. Follow each challenging period with a corresponding recovery period to recharge your batteries.

HABIT #40: STRENGTHEN YOUR MOTIVATION. HAVE SEVERAL MOTIVATORS.

When establishing new goals, do you spend a lot of time figuring out your top motivators or play it by ear, assuming that if you're motivated to act now, you'll be motivated in the future, too? If you do think about your motivations, do you limit yourself to superficial reasons (more money, better looks, etc.) or think about internal rewards you can get, too?

For each new goal, figure out a bigger purpose than just the first reason that comes to your mind. This additional motivational element can make or break your resolutions. In times of doubt, you need all the help you can get to keep going. If your primary, or sole motivator is about impressing somebody, you're in trouble.

Write down all of your motivators: external rewards, internal rewards, and the positive impact you'll have on other people. *Revise them periodically to remind yourself why you're making sacrifices.*

For additional accountability, you can rally other people around your purpose. For example, publicly share your efforts in losing weight to run a marathon and fundraise money for a cause you care about.

HABIT #41: CREATE URGENCY. SET SHORT DEADLINES.

According to the Parkinson's law, work expands to fill the time available for its completion. If you need to prepare a report for next Monday, it will take you exactly until Monday to get it done. If you suddenly need to be ready on Friday, you'll get it done by Friday.

Creating urgency boosts your self-discipline because with limited time available to perform a given task, you can't afford to dilly-dally. You can't procrastinate. *You can't obsess about every single unimportant detail.*

When planning tasks, set deadlines that are shorter than you're comfortable with. This way, you'll harness the power of urgency to improve your productivity and strengthen your self-discipline. Be aware that too much pressure may lead to burnout, though, so periodically take your foot off the pedal.

HABIT #42: GET MOTIVATED TO ACT NOW. THINK OF YOUR DEATH

Next time you're out in the public, look around. Unless we invent some mind-blowing technology, everyone around you will be replaced by completely different people in 150 years.

Why so morbid? Because this exercise can help you live a better life.

You can feel sad about imminent death, or you can use it to your advantage by cheerfully reminding yourself that you're still in control over how your life will unfold.

One day it will all be gone, but while you're still capable of influencing your life, why not make the most of it? Periodically thinking about your death can serve as a powerful reminder to overcome procrastination and introduce positive urgency in your life.

You can use this type of visualization to feel more appreciative. *Even if things aren't going entirely well, you're still alive and still have a say in what your life will be like.*

As an additional exercise, imagine your funeral and ask yourself what you'd like other people to say about you. Do your current choices lead in this direction or elsewhere? *What can you do now to ensure that your legacy is lasting?*

HABIT #43: ENJOY THE JOURNEY. MAKE IT FUN.

Working on your goals doesn't have to be a chore. You don't have to love everything about the process, but if you can make it at least somewhat enjoyable, you'll need less self-discipline to see your objectives through.

If you're working on a boring, repetitive task, play a game in which the objective is to get the task done as quickly as possible. If you want to exercise more often, don't limit yourself to the most common options. Explore different sports and activities. *Make things more fun by doing them with other people.*

Experiment and mix things up to revive your motivation and avoid getting stuck in a rut. A healthy diet doesn't have to consist of the same foods. Building your savings doesn't have to be about scrimping. *Developing a new skill doesn't have to be about reading boring books and rote learning.*

Whatever you can do to make the process more enjoyable is worth trying. The less dependent you are on willpower to work on your objectives, the easier it will be to accomplish your goals.

HABIT #44: STORE YOUR KNOWLEDGE. KEEP A PROGRESS LOG.

Keeping a progress log by jotting down your observations and lessons and revising it regularly will help you learn more efficiently and avoid committing the same mistakes over and over.

One powerful use of a progress log is for improving your diet. You can note how satiated you felt after a meal, how bad you felt after indulging in unhealthy foods, or jot down any other useful tips that help you keep going.

You can also keep a log of your workouts, a log of fighting against a bad habit, a log of your sleep schedule, or a log of a skill you'd like to acquire. *Document your results and frequently go back to your previous entries to memorize important lessons and draw inspiration to keep going.*

93

HABIT #45: BE RELIABLE. KEEP YOUR WORD.

If you often back out of promises, not only do you become unreliable in the eyes of others, but also yourself. *If you don't honor promises made to other people, how likely are you to honor the ones made to yourself?*

Not keeping your word reduces self-trust and makes you less likely to carry on with your goals. *Follow through with all your promises, no matter if to others or yourself.*

For example, if you promised yourself that you wouldn't eat any processed food today, then no matter how much you crave it, make good on your promise. When setting new goals, write and print contracts with yourself. Sign them and keep them somewhere where you can see them. Be punctual—punctuality is about keeping your word, too.

Repeatedly fulfilling promises made to yourself or others will help you build a new identity of a reliable—and by extension, disciplined—person.

HABIT #46: BE FLEXIBLE.
STRETCH AND MOBILIZE.

There's a link between stretching, mobility exercises and self-discipline. It takes willpower to maintain an uncomfortable stretch or consistently, over many weeks, improve your mobility inch by inch. While you work on your flexibility, you simultaneously push your physical limits, restore proper balance in your body, and get stronger mentally.

Foam rolling, applying pressure to certain body parts to relieve tension and alleviate pain, is another habit you should add to your schedule. A double lacrosse ball and a single lacrosse ball is all you need to effectively foam roll all of the most important muscles of your body.

The easiest way to implement the habit of stretching and performing mobility work is to do it immediately after your workout. If you're particularly tense, visit a manual therapist who will skillfully release tension you might otherwise struggle to eliminate by yourself.

HABIT #47: DON'T HESITATE. BE DECISIVE.

Whenever you waver, you waste time and energy. To avoid wasting your resources, form a habit that you don't spend more than a minute on a decision with little significance.

Practice your decisiveness in everyday situations. For example, at the restaurant, pick the first dish you like. Don't waste hours choosing what to wear. Have several universal outfits prepared and go with the first one you like. When buying something inconsequential like paper towel, don't compare multiple options.

Establish simple rules that eliminate decision-making. For example, if a book that sounds interesting and has mostly positive reviews costs less than $10, buy it outright.

Save time and energy on decisions that don't change much and you'll have more resources at your disposal to deal with decisions that do matter.

HABIT #48: TAKE TINY STEPS. BUILD MINI HABITS.

Use mini habits as a way to dip in your toes before you commit to a big change. There's no need to completely revamp your diet right away. *You can start small, see how you feel, and if you like the results, keep going.*

Let's imagine that you want to exercise for thirty minutes every day. You've been procrastinating on this habit for months already. Time is scarce and your energy limited.

Instead of committing to such a big habit right away, start with a mini habit. Exercise for just five minutes a day. Still too much? How about exercising for just one minute? Can you do that? If it still feels too challenging, how about thirty seconds?

Your only objective is to get started. *No matter how small it is, at least you're still getting started*—and that's something that might never happen if you keep waiting for good conditions to start with your original goal.

Once you stick to a mini habit for a few weeks, you'll realize that you can probably add a few minutes to every session. Soon, you'll squeeze in ten minutes of exercise a day. Then you'll notice that twenty minutes is possible, too. Even if it takes you several months, eventually you'll work up to your initial habit.

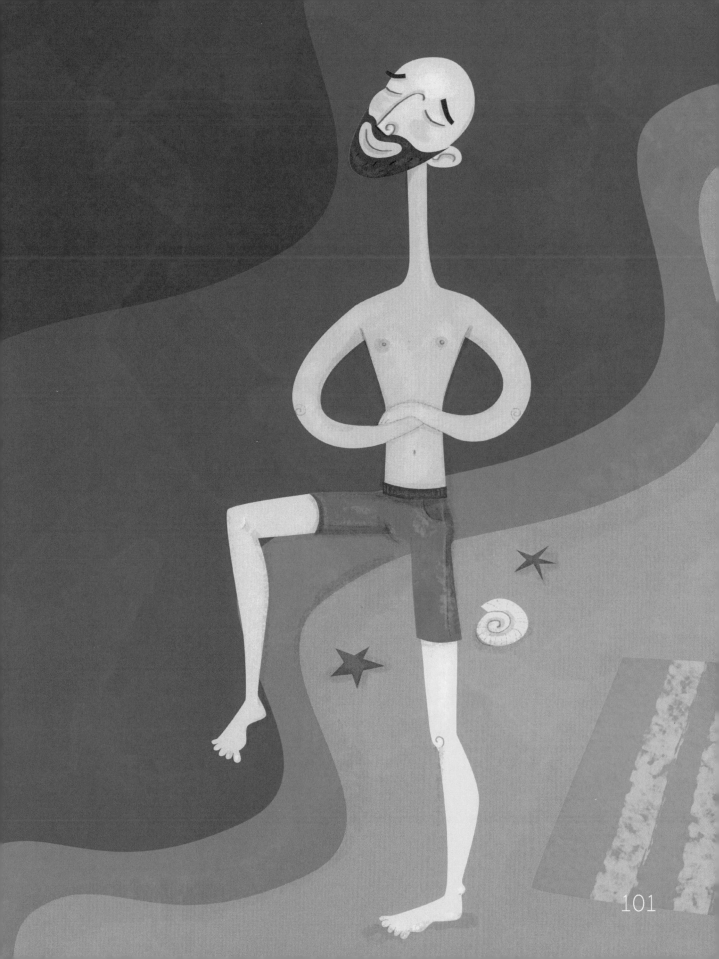

HABIT #49: LEARN EMOTIONAL CONTROL. AGREE TO DISAGREE.

By far one of the most difficult willpower challenges is to end a heated argument before it gets out of control. Understandably, for some topics people are willing to go to great lengths to persuade others. Unfortunately, this approach is never productive. **You may be right beyond any doubt, but no matter how hard you try, you won't change the opinion of another person by brute force.**

And if it's such an unproductive undertaking, why bother? **If you find yourself in an argument, pause for a second and ask yourself: what's my goal here?** Would I change my mind if somebody attacked me the same way?

Take a deep breath and agree to disagree. If the other person escalates, politely insist on changing the topic. If this fails, maintain your composure and walk away.

The ability to control your emotions is one of the most valuable skills you can develop for more happiness in life. From now on, look at every argument as an opportunity to take the high road and gracefully end it, with your emotions contained, your reputation unharmed, and your self-discipline strengthened.

HABIT #50: CREATE YOUR FUTURE. VISUALIZE.

To make something happen, you need to believe it can happen. Visualizing your future turns the improbable dream you have in your head into a clear mental image that will turn into reality if you carry on.

Each morning, visualize yourself as a person who accomplished your goals. Imagine what your everyday life looks like. Think about decisions and sacrifices your future self made to get where they are. Visualize the habits they have, the skills they possess, and the traits they exhibit.

Make it real in your mind and follow this vision with real-world actions. Visualization will help you strengthen the belief that you can change your life and give you more clarity regarding choices you need to make to get to your destination.

EPILOGUE

Fifty habits later we're here, at the end of our journey. While this book ends here, your story has only just started. You can take it in whichever direction you want.

I hope that you not only discovered ideas that will help you make your life better, but that you also enjoyed the illustrations and that they inspired you to take action.

Could you please help spread the message about the life-changing power of self-discipline?

Show this book to your family and friends. Talk about the importance of self-discipline with your kids. Lead by example and strive to be better in all areas of your life.

Habit by habit, leave your own mark on the world. Demonstrate with your own results that embracing self-discipline pays and is key to a fulfilling, successful life. Don't forget to express gratitude and enjoy the process of never-ending personal growth!

DOWNLOAD ANOTHER BOOK FOR FREE

I want to thank you for buying my book and offer you another book (just as valuable as this one): *Grit: How to Keep Going When You Want to Give Up*, completely free.

Visit the link below to receive it:
http://www.profoundselfimprovement.com/il

In Grit, I'll tell you exactly how to stick to your goals, using proven methods from peak performers and science.

In addition to getting Grit, you'll also have an opportunity to get my new books for free, enter giveaways, and receive other valuable emails from me.

Again, here's the link to sign up:

http://www.profoundselfimprovement.com/il

COULD YOU HELP?

Please post your review wherever you bought the book or share your thoughts about it on your favorite social media site.

I'd love to hear your opinion about my book. In the world of book publishing, there are few things more valuable than honest reviews from a wide variety of readers.

Your review will help other readers find out whether my book is for them. It will also help me reach more readers by increasing the visibility of my book.

ABOUT MARTIN MEADOWS

Martin Meadows is a bestselling personal development author, writing about self-discipline and its transformative power to help you become successful and live a more fulfilling life. With a straight-to-the point approach, he is passionate about sharing tips, habits and resources for self-improvement through a combination of science-backed research and personal experience.

Embracing self-control helped Martin overcome extreme shyness, build successful businesses, learn multiple languages, become a bestselling author, and more. As a lifelong learner, he enjoys exploring the limits of his comfort zone through often extreme experiments and adventures involving various sports and wild or exotic places.

Martin uses a pen name. It helps him focus on serving the readers through writing, without the distractions of seeking recognition. He doesn't believe in branding himself as an infallible expert (which he is not), opting instead to offer suggestions and solutions as a fellow personal growth experimenter, with all of the associated failures and successes.

You can read his books here:
http://www.amazon.com/author/martinmeadows.

© *Copyright 2018 by Meadows Publishing. All rights reserved.*

Reproduction in whole or in part of this publication without express written consent is strictly prohibited. The author greatly appreciates you taking the time to read his work. Please consider leaving a review wherever you bought the book, or telling your friends about it, to help us spread the word. Thank you for supporting our work.

Efforts have been made to ensure that the information in this book is accurate and complete. However, the author and the publisher do not warrant the accuracy of the information, text, and graphics contained within the book due to the rapidly changing nature of science, research, known and unknown facts, and the Internet. The author and the publisher do not accept any responsibility for errors, omissions or contrary interpretation of the subject matter herein. This book is presented solely for motivational and informational purposes only.

Illustrated by Tamara Antonijevic.